Belinda Jeffery's

pasta
perfection

C O O K I N G   C L A S S

pasta *perfection*

HINKLER BOOKS

pasta
perfection

Food Editor
Jody Vassallo

Creative Director
Sam Grimmer

Project Editor
Lara Morcombe

First published in 2004 by Hinkler Books Pty Ltd
17–23 Redwood Drive
Dingley, VIC 3172 Australia
www.hinklerbooks.com
Reprinted.2004

ISBN: 1 74121 542 0
EAN: 9 781741 215427

Printed and bound in China

contents

an introduction to pasta

With great ease, pasta can be transformed into low cost, versatile, healthy and tasty meals. For a quiet night at home, dinner can be as simple as tossing a garlic and tomato sauce through spaghetti. An impressive meal of fresh seafood on pappardelle with a creamy saffron sauce can be served to dinner party guests. Or the salad table at a barbecue can be enriched with a hot or cold pasta salad laden with fresh herbs and roasted bell peppers.

pasta shapes

In Italy, pasta is available in hundreds of exciting shapes. Most pasta is known by its Italian name. The literal translation of these names can hint at a pasta's shape: cannelloni or tubes; conchigle or conch shells; fusilli or spindles; gemelli or twins; linguine or little tongues; penne or quills; ravioli or turnips; spaghetti or strings; tagliatelle or ribbons; tortellini or tarts; and vermicelli or little worms.

what shape when?

Choosing the right pasta for a sauce is a common dilemma. Fortunately, there are no hard and fast rules. A good guide is to remember that hollow tube pastas such as penne and rigatoni are good for chunky thicker sauces while thinner flatter pastas such as linguine and fettuccine are better suited to smoother creamy sauces.

fresh or dried?

Most of the recipes in this book call for dried pasta but fresh pasta can be used instead. Fresh pasta will usually absorb more of the sauce than dried pasta so you will need to take this into consideration as it can become quite soggy when served with a wet tomato sauce, but is perfect when tossed with a simple pesto. Fresh pasta tends to be softer than dried so it will not hold its shape when cooked. For this reason it would be better to choose dried pasta for chunkier seafood or vegetable sauces.

flours

Pasta is made by combining flour with water; often it will be enriched with oil or egg. Look for durum wheat pasta as it is considered to be the finest quality flour for pasta making. If you are intolerant to gluten there is a large variety of rice, potato, corn and buckwheat pastas available in the health section of your supermarket or from the local health food store.

storage

Dried pasta will last for up to 6 months stored in an airtight container away from direct sunlight. Fresh pasta can be stored in the refrigerator for up to 5 days or it can be frozen for up to 4 months if securely wrapped in a double layer of plastic. Do not thaw before cooking, simply add straight to the pan from the freezer.

quantities

How much pasta should you cook? As a rule men will usually eat more than women, and adults more than children. However, it is always better to serve too much rather than too little. The following is an approximation of quantities of uncooked pasta per person:

appetizers

fresh pasta 60–80 g per person
dried pasta 90–100 g per person

entrées

fresh pasta 100–125 g per person
dried pasta 125–150 g per person

cooking pasta

Pasta is easy to cook. Firstly, you need a good-sized pot for boiling the water. If the pot is too small, the pasta will stick together and glue itself to the bottom of the pan. If you choose to cook your pasta in salted water, don't add the salt until the water has boiled as unsalted water will reach boiling point much faster. Covering the pot will also help it to boil quicker. Once the water has boiled,

add the pasta and stir it a couple of times to start the pasta moving in the water. Cover the pan and allow it to return to the boil. Remove the lid as soon as it reaches the boil or the water will overflow onto the stovetop.

Cook the pasta until it is al dente, which is Italian for "the tooth". It should be soft but still slightly firm. Once cooked, drain the pasta in a large metal colander. There is no need to rinse it under cold water unless it is going to be used to make pasta salad. Do not over drain the pasta, as this will make it sticky. Pasta should be served as soon as it has been cooked – if left to stand it will form a solid mass. If you are making a pasta salad and need to cool the pasta, toss through a little olive oil to keep the pasta separate. It is best to prepare the sauce before you cook the pasta.

The cooking time will vary depending on the brand, so be sure to read the manufacturer's instructions. Fresh pasta takes less time to cook than dried and should not be overcooked or it will break up. Fresh gnocchi will float to the surface of the pot when it is cooked and it should be removed from the pan using a slotted spoon.

vegetarian

pasta with squash and sage butter

ingredients

2 tablespoons olive oil
2 cloves garlic, minced
2 tablespoon chopped fresh sage
1 butternut squash, cut into large dice
400 g (13 oz) dried penne
salt and black pepper
90 g (3 oz) butter
30 g (1 oz) pine nuts kernels
30 g (1 oz) parmesan, grated
extra sage to garnish
serves 4

1 Preheat oven to 230°C (450°F, gas mark 8). Combine oil, garlic, 1 tablespoon of sage and the butternut squash. Cook in oven for 20 minutes until tender.

2 Cook pasta in a large pan of boiling water, until al dente, drain, reserving 1 cup of water.

3 Melt butter in a large skillet, add remaining chopped sage, cook gently for 2–3 minutes. Put pine nuts on a baking tray, place in oven and toast until golden.

4 Add the reserved cooking liquid to the butter. Add pasta and cooked squash. Toss and serve sprinkled with the parmesan, pine nuts and pepper. Garnish with fresh sage.

preparation time
15 minutes

cooking time
30 minutes

nutritional value per serve
fat: 10.7 g
carbohydrate: 23 g
protein: 6 g

1 Preheat oven to 200°C (400°F, gas mark 6). Cook pasta in a large pan of boiling water, until al dente, and drain. Return to pan, toss with half the butter and half the parmesan. Add gruyère, bel paese, mozzarella and pepper, mix well to combine.

2 Transfer pasta and cheese mixture to a greased ovenproof dish. Dot with remaining butter. Sprinkle with remaining parmesan. Bake for 10–15 minutes, until top is crisp and golden. Leave to stand for 15 minutes before serving.

wholewheat spaghetti with four cheeses

ingredients

400 g (13 oz) dried wholewheat spaghetti
salt and black pepper
90 g (3 oz) butter
60 g (2 oz) parmesan, grated
90 g (3 oz) gruyère, cut into thin strips
90 g (3 oz) bel paese, cut into thin strips
125 g (4 oz) mozzarella, cut into chunks
serves 4

i

preparation time
20 minutes

cooking time
25 minutes, plus
15 minutes
standing

**nutritional value
per serve**
fat: 21.7 g
carbohydrate: 28 g
protein: 16.1 g

penne with bell peppers and mascarpone

ingredients

2 tablespoons olive oil
1 clove garlic, minced
2 red onions, chopped
1 green bell peppers, chopped
1 red bell peppers, chopped
1 yellow bell peppers, chopped
400 g (13 oz) dried penne
200 g (7 oz) mascarpone
juice of ½ lemon
4 tablespoons chopped flat-leaf parsley
black pepper
4 tablespoons grated parmesan (optional)
serves 4

1 Heat oil in large skillet. Cook garlic, onions and bell peppers for 5–10 minutes on medium low heat, stirring frequently, until vegetables have softened. Cook pasta in a large pan of boiling water, until al dente. Drain and set aside.

2 Add half the mascarpone, the lemon juice, parsley and seasoning to the pepper mixture. Stir to combine. Cook on medium heat until mascarpone melts.

3 Add remaining mascarpone to pasta, mix to combine. Pour pepper mixture into pasta, toss well. Serve sprinkled with parmesan.

preparation time
10 minutes

cooking time
15 minutes

**nutritional value
per serve**
fat: 14.3 g
carbohydrate: 26 g
protein: 5.6 g

pappardelle with shallots and peas

ingredients

100 g (3½ oz) butter
200 ml (7 fl oz) vegetable or chicken stock
4 tablespoons finely chopped shallots
12 iceberg lettuce leaves, shredded
315 g (10 oz) fresh peas, shelled
500 g (1 lb) fresh pappardelle
2 tablespoons chopped fresh mint
salt and pepper
parmesan, grated
serves 4

preparation time
10 minutes

cooking time
15 minutes

nutritional value per serve
fat: 7 g
carbohydrate: 29 g
protein: 6.7 g

1 Heat half the butter, 2 tablespoons of stock and shallots in a small pan. Cook, covered over a medium heat for 5 minutes or until the shallots have softened, stirring occasionally. Add lettuce leaves and cook, stirring for 2 minutes.

2 Add peas and half the remaining stock to pan, bring to the boil, reduce heat and cook, covered, for 7 minutes or until the peas are tender. Add a little more stock if the sauce dries out. Season with salt and pepper to taste.

3 Cook pasta in a large pan of boiling water, until al dente. Drain well. Toss through the remaining butter in a serving bowl, spoon over the sauce. Sprinkle with mint and serve with parmesan.

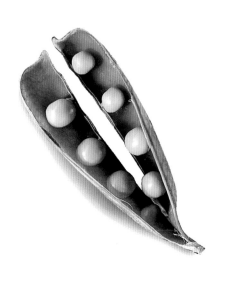

thick minestrone with pesto

ingredients

3 tablespoons olive oil
1 onion, chopped
2 cloves garlic, minced
1 potato, cut into large dice
2 small carrots, cubed
1 large small zucchini, cut into dice
$1/4$ white cabbage, chopped
700 ml ($1^{1}/_{4}$ pints) vegetable stock
2 x 400 g (13 oz) cans tomatoes, chopped
75 g ($2^{1}/_{2}$ oz) pasta shells
salt and black pepper
4 tablespoons grated parmesan
4 tablespoons pesto
serves 4

preparation time
15 minutes

cooking time
45 minutes

nutritional value per serve
fat: 3.9 g
carbohydrate: ?
protein: 2 g

1 Place oil in a large pan, add onion, garlic, potato, carrots, zucchini and cabbage. Cook for 5–7 minutes, until softened.

2 Add stock and tomatoes and bring to the boil. Reduce heat and simmer for 20 minutes, add pasta shells and seasoning. Cook for a further 10 minutes, until pasta is al dente. Divide soup between bowls and top each serving with a tablespoon of parmesan and pesto.

penne with mushrooms and dolcelatte

ingredients

2 tablespoons olive oil
1 small leek, thinly sliced
8 bacon slices, thinly chopped
250 g (8 oz) button mushrooms, chopped
$\frac{1}{2}$ cup (125 ml, 4 fl oz) white wine or stock
500 g (1 lb) fresh penne
200 g (7 oz) dolcelatte, chopped
salt and black pepper
fresh flat-leaf parsley to garnish
serves 4

1 Heat oil in a skillet. Cook leek on medium high heat for 3–4 minutes, until softened. Add bacon and cook until golden.

2 Add mushrooms, cook for 3–4 minutes, stirring occasionally. Stir in wine, or stock, reduce heat and simmer for 2–3 minutes, until reduced.

3 Cook pasta in a large pan of boiling water, until al dente. Drain well and add to mushroom mixture with the dolcelatte. Stir gently for 1–2 minutes. Season with salt and pepper and garnish with parsley.

preparation time
10 minutes

cooking time
20 minutes

nutritional value per serve
fat: 6.5 g
carbohydrate: 22.5 g
protein: 10.6 g

stortelli with bell peppers and eggplant

ingredients

¹/₂ cup (125 ml, 4 fl oz) extra virgin olive oil
2 cloves garlic, minced
1 eggplant, peeled and
   cut into large dice
1 red bell pepper, chopped
1 yellow bell pepper, chopped
425 g (14 oz) can chopped tomatoes
¹/₂ cup (125 ml, 4 fl oz) dry white wine
salt and black pepper
400 g (13 oz) dried stortelli
2 tablespoons chopped fresh oregano
70 g (2¹/₄ oz) pitted black olives, sliced
serves 4

i

preparation time
15 minutes

cooking time
25 minutes

**nutritional value
per serve**
fat: 7.7 g
carbohydrate: 20.6 g
protein: 3.8 g

1 Heat oil in a large pan. Add garlic, cook for 1 minute on a medium heat, stirring. Add eggplant and bell peppers. Cook, uncovered, stirring frequently, for 5 minutes or until just browned.

2 Add tomatoes and cook for 4–5 minutes, stirring frequently, until liquid has reduced slightly. Pour in wine, bring to the boil, and season with salt and pepper. Reduce heat and cook partially covered for 20 minutes.

3 Cook pasta in a large pan of boiling water, until al dente. Drain. Transfer to a serving bowl and pour over sauce. Garnish with oregano and olives.

magpie's nest

ingredients

150 g (5 oz) dried macaroni
4 tablespoons crème fraîche
1 teaspoon brown sugar
1 teaspoon lemon juice
1 teaspoon light soy sauce
1 tablespoon chopped fresh parsley
black pepper
2 teaspoons vegetable oil
250 g (8 oz) turkey breast steak, cut
   into thin strips
1 teaspoon mild mustard
1 carrot, julienned
1 small zucchini, julienned
extra parsley to garnish

serves 2

i

preparation time
15 minutes

cooking time
20 minutes

**nutritional value
per serve**
fat: 6.3 g
carbohydrate: 17 g
protein: 14.3 g

1 Cook macaroni in a large pan of boiling water, until al dente. Drain well.

2 In a large bowl, mix crème fraîche, sugar, lemon juice, soy sauce and parsley until combined. Season, cover and refrigerate. Heat oil in a large skillet or wok, add turkey strips and mustard and cook for 5 minutes, tossing frequently until turkey is cooked through.

3 Add carrot and zucchini, cook for 4 minutes or until tender but crunchy. Stir in the macaroni and heat through. Add crème fraîche mixture and cook for 1 minute, stirring to combine. Garnish with parsley to serve.

fusilli with bell peppers and sun-dried tomatoes

ingredients

1 large red bell pepper
1 large yellow bell pepper
½ cup (125 ml, 4 fl oz) extra virgin olive oil
2 shallots, finely chopped
1 clove garlic, minced
1 teaspoon dried chilli peppers, crushed
½ cup (125 ml, 4 fl oz) vegetable stock
125 g (4 oz) sun-dried tomatoes in oil, drained and chopped
2 tablespoons capers, rinsed and dried
2 tablespoons balsamic vinegar
400 g (13 oz) dried fusilli
2 tablespoons chopped fresh oregano
serves 4

1 Preheat broiler to high. Broil bell peppers until skin blackens and blisters. Transfer to a plastic bag to cool, remove skins and seeds and chop.

2 Heat half the oil in a large pan, add shallots and cook for 5 minutes until softened. Add garlic, chilli peppers and 2 tablespoons of the stock. Cook for 5 minutes, add bell peppers and sun-dried tomatoes. Cook for a further 10 minutes, adding more stock if needed. Stir in capers and vinegar and cook for 1 minute.

3 Cook pasta in a large pan of boiling water, until al dente. Drain and toss with remaining oil. Spoon over the sauce, mix to combine. Serve hot or cold, garnished with oregano.

preparation time
15 minutes

cooking time
45 minutes

nutritional value per serve
fat: 11.5 g
carbohydrate: 29 g
protein: 6.2 g

pasta with goat cheese and asparagus

ingredients

1 tablespoon sunflower oil
2 tablespoons butter
2 red onions, thinly sliced
1 clove garlic, minced
sea salt and freshly ground black pepper
400 g (13 oz) dried pasta, such as penne
250 g (8 oz) bunch asparagus, trimmed
  and cut into small pieces
150 g (5 oz) peas, fresh or frozen
100 g (3¹/₂ oz) goat cheese, crumbled
serves 4

1 Heat oil and butter in a skillet, cook onion over a medium heat for 7 minutes, stirring occasionally. Add garlic and cook for a further 3 minutes, until golden and crisp.

2 Bring a large pan of water to the boil. Add pasta and cook for 5 minutes, add asparagus and cook for a further 2 minutes, add peas and cook for further 2 minutes. Drain well.

3 Return pasta and vegetables to the pan, add most of the onion. Add goat cheese, sea salt and black pepper, mix to combine. Serve topped with the remaining onions.

preparation time
15 minutes

cooking time
20 minutes

**nutritional value
per serve**
fat: 6.3 g
carbohydrate: 27 g
protein: 7.1 g

fusilli with tomato sauce

ingredients

2 x 425 g (14 oz) cans chopped tomatoes
2 teaspoons tomato puree
1 teaspoon sugar
2 onions, chopped
2 stalks celery, chopped
½ cup (125 ml, 4 fl oz) extra virgin olive oil
salt and black pepper
4 tablespoons butter
400 g (13 oz) dried fusilli (pasta twists)

serves 4

preparation time
15 minutes

cooking time
45 minutes

nutritional value per serve
fat: 9.3 g
carbohydrate: 24 g
protein: 4.5 g

1 Place tomatoes in a large pan, add tomato puree, sugar, onions, celery, oil, salt and pepper. Cook on a medium high heat for 8–10 minutes until softened. Remove from heat, allow to cool. In a food processor combine until pureed.

2 Return to pan, heat and add wine. Reduce heat, simmer for 20 minutes or until thickened. Add butter and stir until melted and combined. Add more salt and pepper if desired.

3 Cook pasta in a large pan of boiling water, until al dente. Drain, pour over the sauce, toss well and serve.

pasta primavera

ingredients

4 tablespoons butter
225 g (7½ oz) baby spinach
300 g (10 oz) fresh peas
300 g (10 oz) fava beans
salt and black pepper
4 tablespoons crème fraîche
1 bunch green onions, finely chopped
2 tablespoons finely chopped
  fresh parsley
90 g (3 oz) parmesan, grated
400 g (13 oz) dried penne
serves 4

1 Melt butter in a pan, add spinach, cover, and cook for 2–3 minutes on medium high heat until wilted. Set aside to cool. Cook peas and beans in boiling water for 5 minutes, until tender. Drain and set aside.

2 Process spinach and crème fraîche in a food processor until smooth. Return puree to the pan, stir in peas and beans. Stir in green onions and parsley. Season and add half the parmesan. Keep warm over a low heat.

3 Cook pasta in a large pan of boiling water, until al dente. Drain, toss with spinach sauce. Sprinkle with the remaining parmesan.

preparation time
15 minutes

cooking time
20 minutes

nutritional value per serve
fat: 7.7 g
carbohydrate: 21 g
protein: 8.8 g

vegetarian lasagne

ingredients

250 g (8 oz) instant lasagne sheets
200 g (7 oz) ricotta cheese
250 g (8 oz) mozzarella, grated
2 tablespoons oil
1 large eggplant
125 g (4 oz) mushrooms, sliced
1 carrot, grated
1 small zucchini, grated
500 g (1 lb) jar pasta sauce
140 g (4^1/$_2$ oz) tomato paste
1 cup (250 ml, 8 fl oz) water
^{1}/$_2$ cup (125 ml, 4 fl oz) red wine
2 tablespoons chopped fresh parsley
serves 4–6

1 Preheat oven to 190°C (375°F, gas mark 5). In a large pan, heat oil, add eggplant, mushrooms, carrot and zucchini and cook on a medium-high heat for 2–3 minutes. Stir in pasta sauce, tomato paste, water, wine and parsley. Cover, reduce heat and simmer for 15 minutes, stirring occasionally.

i

preparation time
30 minutes

cooking time
1 hour, plus
10 minutes
standing

**nutritional value
per serve**
fat: 5.9 g
carbohydrate: 12 g
protein: 6.2 g

2 Butter an 8 x 12 inch ovenproof dish and spread ^{1}/$_3$ of vegetable sauce over bottom. Cover with a layer of lasagne sheets. Spread ^{1}/$_3$ of ricotta onto pasta and sprinkle with ^{1}/$_3$ cup mozzarella.

3 Repeat the layers twice, finishing with ricotta and sprinkling with cup of mozzarella cheese.

4 Bake for 30–40 minutes, until golden and bubbling. Allow to stand for 10 minutes before serving.

linguine with leeks and mushrooms

preparation time
20 minutes

cooking time
20 minutes

nutritional value per serve
fat: 3.1 g
carbohydrate: 20 g
protein: 5.6 g

ingredients

500 g (1 lb) leeks, sliced
275 g (9 oz) button mushrooms, sliced
1 bay leaf
40 g (1½ oz) butter
40 g (1½ oz) all purpose flour
2 cups (500 ml, 16 fl oz) milk
2 tablespoons finely chopped fresh chives
500 g (1 lb) fresh linguine or tagliatelle
extra chives to garnish

serves 4–6

1 Steam leeks, mushrooms and bay leaf over a large pan of boiling water for 5–10 minutes, until tender. Discard bay leaf and keep vegetables warm.

2 Melt butter in a large pan, add flour and cook gently for 1 minute, stirring. Remove from heat and gradually add milk. Return to heat, bring to boil, stirring, until thickened. Reduce heat and simmer for 2 minutes, stirring. Add reserved vegetables, chives and black pepper, heat through.

3 Cook pasta in a large pan of boiling water, until al dente, and drain well. Return to pan, add leek and mushroom sauce and toss lightly to combine. Garnish with fresh chives.

gnocchi with thyme

ingredients

500 g (1 lb) fresh potato gnocchi
3 tablespoons olive oil
100 g (3½ oz) butter
15 g (½ oz) fresh thyme leaves
3 tablespoons chopped fresh parsley
55 g (2 oz) roasted pecans or walnuts
1 red bell pepper

serves 4

i

preparation time
15 minutes

cooking time
25 minutes

nutritional value per serve
fat: 20.8 g
carbohydrate: 17 g
protein: 3.7 g

1 Preheat broiler to high. Heat oil in a large pan until very hot. Add gnocchi, cook gently until golden brown. Drain on paper towels and set aside.

2 Cut bell pepper into 4 and press flat onto broiling rack, skin side up. Cook until skin blisters and blackens. Remove, place in a plastic bag and seal until cool. Remove skin and cut into strips.

3 Heat butter in a large pan, add herbs and sauté for 1 minute. Add gnocchi and pecans (or walnuts), toss to heat through. Serve topped with char-grilled bell peppers.

warm italian pasta shell salad

ingredients

175 g (6 oz) dried pasta shells
150 g (5 oz) small green beans, halved
4 green onions, sliced
1 green bell pepper, chopped
125 g (4 oz) cherry tomatoes, halved
1 large avocado, chopped
black pepper
fresh basil leaves
dressing
3 tablespoons olive oil
1 tablespoon white-wine vinegar
1 tablespoon clear honey
1 teaspoon dijon mustard
serves 4

1 Cook the pasta shells until almost cooked. Add beans and cook for 2 minutes or until al dente. Drain well.

2 Place pasta and beans in a large bowl with the green onions, green bell pepper, cherry tomatoes, avocado and seasoning.

3 To make the dressing, place oil, vinegar, honey and mustard in a jar, shake well to combine. Pour dressing over pasta and toss. Garnish with basil leaves.

i

preparation time
15 minutes

cooking time
20 minutes

**nutritional value
per serve**
fat: 12.2 g
carbohydrate: 16 g
protein: 3.4 g

meat

spaghetti carbonara

ingredients

185 g (6 oz) sliced ham, cut into strips
4 eggs
1/3 cup (90 ml, 3 fl oz) single cream
90 g (3 oz) parmesan, grated
500 g (1 lb) dried spaghetti
freshly ground black pepper
serves 4

i

preparation time
15 minutes

cooking time
20 minutes

**nutritional value
per serve**
fat: 9.5 g
carbohydrate: 40 g
protein: 15.2 g

1 Heat a nonstick skillet and cook ham on a medium heat for 2–3 minutes. Place eggs, cream and parmesan in a large bowl and beat lightly to combine. Set aside.

2 Cook spaghetti in a large pan of boiling water, until al dente. Place spaghetti in a large serving dish while still hot, add egg mixture and ham and toss, allowing the heat of the spaghetti to cook the sauce. Season with black pepper and serve.

tagliatelle with bolognese

ingredients

3 tablespoons olive oil

2 tablespoons butter

115 g (4 oz) pancetta or bacon, roughly chopped

1 small onion, finely diced

1 small carrot, finely diced

1 stalk celery, finely diced

1 clove garlic, minced

400 g (13 oz) ground beef

$\frac{1}{2}$ cup (125 ml, 4 fl oz) dry white wine

2 tablespoons tomato puree

$\frac{1}{2}$ cup (125 ml, 4 fl oz) beef stock

500 g (1 lb) fresh tagliatelle

parmesan, grated

serves 4

preparation time
20 minutes

cooking time
2 hours
50 minutes

**nutritional value
per serve**
fat: 9.1 g
carbohydrate: 22 g
protein: 10.7 g

1 Place oil, butter, pancetta or bacon, onion, carrot, celery and garlic in a large pan and cook over a low heat for 5–7 minutes, until vegetables have softened, stirring occasionally. Add ground beef and cook for 3–5 minutes, until browned.

2 Add wine and boil for 2–3 minutes, until reduced by more than half. Mix in tomato puree, stock and salt and pepper. Return to the boil, reduce heat and simmer, uncovered for 2–2½ hours, stirring occasionally. Add 2 tablespoons of milk whenever the sauce starts to dry out.

3 Cook pasta in a large pan of boiling water, until al dente. Drain, transfer to a serving bowl and spoon over the sauce. Toss to combine, garnish with parmesan and serve.

penne with bacon and basil

1 Cook penne in a large pan of boiling water, until al dente. Drain, set aside and keep warm.

2 Heat oil in a large skillet and cook garlic over a medium heat for 1 minute. Add bacon and cook for a further 2–3 minutes until bacon is crispy. Add basil, walnuts and penne, season with black pepper and toss to combine. Sprinkle with parmesan and serve.

ingredients

500 g (1 lb) dried penne
1 tablespoon olive oil
2 cloves garlic, minced
6 bacon slices, chopped
2 tablespoons chopped fresh basil
60 g (2 oz) walnuts, chopped
freshly ground black pepper
30 g (1 oz) parmesan, grated
serves 4

preparation time
20 minutes

cooking time
25 minutes

nutritional value per serve
fat: 9.3 g
carbohydrate: 38 g
protein: 13.8 g

ham and cheese tortellini with sage butter

ingredients

90 g (3 oz) butter
1 clove garlic, minced
20 fresh sage leaves, finely chopped,
salt and black pepper
600 g (1¼ lb) fresh ham and cheese
   tortellini
60 g (2 oz) parmesan, grated
extra parmesan to serve
serves 4

1 Melt butter in a small pan, add garlic and sage, and sauté on a low heat for 1–2 minutes. Season with salt and pepper.

2 Cook pasta in a large pan of boiling water, until al dente. Drain and set aside.

3 Place tortellini in a large serving bowl, pour in butter sauce and parmesan, toss well to combine. Garnish with extra parmesan.

preparation time
10 minutes

cooking time
15 minutes

**nutritional value
per serve**
fat: 17.8 g
carbohydrate: 11 g
protein: 11.5 g

3 Melt butter in a large pan, add flour and cook on a low heat for 3 minutes. Add milk, stirring constantly, bring to the boil, reduce heat and simmer for 3–4 minutes until thickened. Add cheese and egg yolks, beating to combine well. Season with salt and pepper. Remove from heat.

4 In a large ovenproof dish, mix penne and meat mixture together. Add 2 eggs, mix to combine. Pour the béchamel sauce over the top, sprinkle with additional cheese, and bake in the oven for 30–45 minutes, until hot and bubbling. Stand for 15 minutes before serving.

pasticcio

1 Heat oil in a large pan, sauté onion on medium high heat for 5 minutes. Add ground beef, cook for 10 minutes, stirring to separate meat as it cooks. Cook pasta in a large pan of boiling water, until al dente. Drain well and set aside. Preheat oven to 180°C (350°F, gas mark 4).

2 Add tomato paste, tomatoes, water, oregano, sugar, worcestershire sauce and the cinnamon stick, bring to the boil, reduce heat and simmer for 45 minutes until thick. Season with salt and pepper.

ingredients

3 tablespoons oil
1 onion, sliced
1 kg (2 lb) ground beef
2 tablespoons tomato paste
425 g (14 oz) can tomatoes
1 cup (250 ml, 8 fl oz) water
2 teaspoons chopped fresh oregano
1 teaspoon sugar
1 tablespoon worcestershire sauce
1 cinnamon stick
salt and pepper
400 g (13 oz) dried penne (quills)
2 whole eggs
béchamel sauce
120 g (4 oz) butter
3 tablespoons flour
1 litre (1²/₃ pints) milk
250 g (8 oz) romano cheese
4 egg yolks
extra 120 g (4 oz) romano cheese, grated
serves 4-6

i

preparation time
15 minutes

cooking time
40 minutes

nutritional value
per serve
fat: 9.9 g
carbohydrate: 9.6 g
protein: 10.9 g

spaghetti with ham and mushrooms

ingredients

3 tablespoons extra virgin olive oil
4 tablespoons butter
100 g (3 1/2 oz) mushrooms, sliced
2 shallots, finely chopped
145 g (5 oz) thick cooked ham, chopped
1 beef bouillon cube
3 tablespoons red wine
4 tablespoons tomato paste
salt and black pepper
500 g (1 lb) fresh spaghetti
parmesan cheese, grated

serves 4

1 Heat oil and butter in a large skillet. Add mushrooms, shallots and ham, fry on medium low heat for 2–3 minutes, until lightly coloured.

2 Add crumbled bouillon cube and wine to mushroom mixture. Simmer

for 1–2 minutes, stir in tomato paste and simmer for further 2–3 minutes. Season to taste.

3 Cook pasta in a large pan of boiling water, until al dente. Drain well, reserving water.

Add 1 cup of reserved water to mushroom mixture. Stir for 1 minute, adding more water if needed. Add pasta to mushroom sauce, mix to combine. Serve with grated parmesan.

i

preparation time
15 minutes

cooking time
20 minutes

nutritional value per serve
fat: 12.9 g
carbohydrate: 34 g
protein: 9.6 g

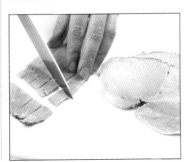

meatballs with spicy tomato sauce

ingredients

50 g (2 oz) fresh white breadcrumbs
500 g (1 lb) ground beef
2 bacon slices, finely chopped
1 onion, chopped
3 tablespoons chopped fresh parsley
1 egg, beaten
sea salt
freshly ground black pepper
2 tablespoons sunflower oil
400 g (13 oz) jar garlic pasta sauce
400 g (13 oz) dried pasta (tagliatelle or penne)
extra parsley to garnish

serves 4

i

preparation time
15 minutes

cooking time
25 minutes

nutritional value per serve
fat: 5.3 g
carbohydrate: 21 g
protein: 11 g

1 Place breadcrumbs in a large bowl, combine with beef, bacon, onion, parsley, egg and salt and pepper, mix well. Roll into 20 balls and flatten slightly with the palm of your hand. Refrigerate for 10 minutes.

2 Heat oil in a skillet and, over a medium-high heat, cook meatballs in batches, until browned on both sides. Drain off excess oil, pour pasta sauce over meatballs. Reduce heat and simmer for 10 minutes, turning occasionally, until cooked through.

3 Cook pasta in boiling water, until al dente, and drain. Serve meatballs with pasta and garnish with extra parsley.

meat ravioli with cream and parmesan

ingredients

600 g (1¼ lb) fresh beef ravioli
salt and black pepper
220 ml (7½ fl oz) heavy cream
2 tablespoons butter
freshly grated nutmeg
60 g (2 oz) parmesan, grated
extra parmesan to serve
serves 4

i

preparation time
10 minutes

cooking time
15 minutes

nutritional value per serve
fat: 16.3 g
carbohydrate: 14 g
protein: 7 g

1 Cook ravioli in a large pan of boiling water, until al dente. Place half the cream and the butter in a large skillet. Heat gently for 1 minute or until butter has melted.

2 Drain ravioli, add immediately to cream and butter mixture. Cook for 30 seconds, stirring. Mix in remaining cream, nutmeg and parmesan. Season and toss for a few seconds, until well combined and heated through. Serve with extra parmesan.

linguine with ham, saffron and cream

ingredients

$^1/_4$ teaspoon saffron strands
220 ml ($7^1/_2$ fl oz) heavy cream
150 g (5 oz) thick sliced ham, cut into large dice
60 g (2 oz) parmesan, grated
black pepper
400 g (13 oz) dried linguine
2 tablespoons chopped fresh parsley
extra parmesan to serve

serves 4

1 Pour 2 tablespoons of boiling water over the saffron and infuse for 10 minutes. Place cream, ham and parmesan in a small saucepan and heat gently – do not allow to boil. Add the saffron mixture to the cream and ham, season with salt and pepper to taste, and mix well.

2 Cook pasta in a large pan of boiling water, until al dente. Drain and transfer to a serving bowl. Pour over the sauce, mixing well to combine, sprinkle with parsley and extra parmesan.

preparation time
15 minutes

cooking time
20 minutes

nutritional value per serve
fat: 15 g
carbohydrate: 33 g
protein: 12.5 g

macaroni with lamb ragoût

ingredients

2 tablespoons olive oil
4 tablespoons butter
1 stalk celery, finely chopped
1 onion, finely chopped
1 small carrot, finely chopped
360 g (12 oz) ground lamb
black pepper
1 cup (250 ml, 8 fl oz) milk
400 g (13 oz) dried macaroni
2 tablespoons chopped fresh mint
parmesan, grated
serves 4

i

preparation time
15 minutes

cooking time
20 minutes

nutritional value
per serve
fat: 11.3 g
carbohydrate: 22 g
protein: 9.9 g

1 Heat oil and butter in a large skillet. Gently fry celery, onion and carrot for 5–7 minutes, until softened. Add lamb and cook, stirring, for 5–6 minutes, until meat has browned. Season.

2 Reduce heat to very low, stir in milk a little at a time, until milk is absorbed with each addition, and mixture is cooked through.

3 Cook pasta in a large pan of boiling water, until al dente. Drain. Garnish with mint and sprinkle with extra parmesan.

gnocchi with pork and bell peppers

ingredients

360 g (12 oz) pork steak, cut into large dice
4 cloves garlic, minced
1 tablespoon dried oregano
juice of 1/2 lemon
1/2 cup (125 ml, 4 fl oz) extra virgin olive oil
salt and black pepper
1 small onion, finely chopped
1/2 stalk celery, finely chopped
3 tablespoons finely chopped fresh parsley
250 g (8 oz) yellow bell peppers, chopped
220 ml (7 1/2 fl oz) tomato paste
3 tablespoons beef stock
800 g (1 lb 10 oz) fresh gnocchi
25 g (1 oz) pitted black olives, sliced

serves 4

i

preparation time
20 minutes

cooking time
30 minutes, plus
1 hour marinating

nutritional value per serve
fat: 7.4 g
carbohydrate: 14 g
protein: 7.4 g

1 Place pork in a shallow, non-metallic dish. Mix in half the garlic, the oregano, lemon juice, 1 tablespoon of oil and salt and pepper. Cover and refrigerate for 1 hour.

2 Heat remaining oil in a large pan. Add onion and a pinch of salt. Cook for 5 minutes until softened. Stir in remaining garlic, celery, parsley and peppers, and cook over a low heat for 10 minutes.

3 Stir in the tomato paste and simmer for a further 10 minutes, stirring often. Add pork, marinade and stock. Simmer, uncovered, for 10 minutes or until thickened and cooked through, stirring occasionally.

4 Cook gnocchi in a large pan of boiling water, until al dente. Drain and transfer to a large serving bowl. Spoon over the sauce and toss to combine. Sprinkle with olives.

tagliatelle with asparagus and prosciutto

ingredients

500 g (1 lb) asparagus
4 tablespoons unsalted butter
2 tablespoons olive oil
1 green onion, sliced
60 g (2 oz) proscuitto, cut into strips
150 ml (5 fl oz) heavy cream
salt and black pepper
500 g (1 lb) fresh tagliatelle
parmesan, grated
serves 4

i

preparation time
10 minutes

cooking time
20 minutes

**nutritional value
per serve**
fat: 13.1 g
carbohydrate: 26 g
protein: 7 g

1 Cut asparagus spears into 1-inch pieces. Heat butter and oil in a large skillet, add green onions, cook for 2 minutes to soften, stir in proscuitto. Cook for 2 minutes, add asparagus and cook for 5 minutes, until softened. Pour in cream and bring to the boil, season to taste.

2 Cook pasta in a large pan of boiling water, until al dente. Drain and transfer to serving bowl, pour over the sauce.

seafood

fresh crab tagliatelle

ingredients

400 g (13 oz) dried tagliatelle
3 tablespoons olive oil
2 cloves garlic, minced
1 red chilli pepper, seeded and chopped
rind (zest) of 1 lemon, finely grated
2 fresh dressed crabs (about 300 g,
10 oz crabmeat)
200 ml (7 fl oz) light cream
1 tablespoon lemon juice
salt and black pepper
2 tablespoons chopped fresh parsley
serves 4

i

preparation time
20 minutes

cooking time
40 minutes

nutritional value
per serve
fat: 11.1 g
carbohydrate: 28 g
protein: 9.2 g

1 Cook pasta in a large pan of boiling water, until al dente. Drain well.

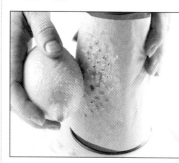

2 Heat oil in a large skillet. Gently fry garlic, chilli pepper and lemon zest for 3–4 minutes, until lightly coloured. Add crabmeat, cream and lemon juice. Simmer for 1–2 minutes and season to taste.

3 Put pasta into serving bowls. Spoon crab mixture over the top and sprinkle with parsley.

flaked tuna pasta salad in tomato dressing

ingredients

225 g (7½ oz) dried wholewheat pasta
  shells or fusilli
4 green onions, sliced
1 yellow bell pepper, chopped
125 g (4 oz) sugar snap peas, chopped
200 g (7 oz) can sweetcorn, drained
185 g (6 oz) can tuna in water, drained
  and flaked

dressing

5 tablespoons tomato paste
1 tablespoon extra virgin olive oil
2 teaspoons balsamic vinegar
pinch of superfine sugar
2 tablespoons fresh basil, chopped
black pepper
extra green onion strips for garnish
serves 4

1 Cook pasta in a large pan of boiling water until al dente. Drain, rinse under cold water, drain thoroughly. Place in serving bowl.

2 Add green onions, yellow bell pepper, sugar snap peas, sweetcorn and tuna, toss lightly. Keep warm.

3 To make the dressing, whisk tomato paste, olive oil, vinegar, sugar, basil and black pepper in a bowl. Mix well. Pour dressing over the pasta. Mix to combine. Garnish with extra green onion.

i

preparation time
15 minutes

cooking time
20 minutes

**nutritional value
per serve**
fat: 2.6 g
carbohydrate: 21 g
protein: 8.6 g

baked penne with tomatoes and anchovies

ingredients

250 g (8 oz) ripe tomatoes
250 g (8 oz) mozzarella, grated
4 tablespoons grated parmesan
55 g (2 oz) cheddar, grated
2 tablespoons dried oregano
4 tablespoons extra virgin olive oil, plus extra for greasing and drizzling
salt and black pepper
2 tablespoons butter
1 small onion, finely chopped
2 garlic cloves, minced
400 g (13 oz) dried penne
4 anchovy fillets, drained and chopped

serves 4

preparation time
20 minutes

cooking time
40 minutes

nutritional value per serve
fat: 17.4 g
carbohydrate: 25 g
protein: 12.9 g

1 Preheat oven to 200°C (400°F, gas mark 6). Put tomatoes into a bowl, cover with boiling water. Leave for 30 seconds, peel, seed and chop. Combine mozzarella, parmesan, cheddar, oregano, 2 tablespoons of oil and season with salt and pepper. Set aside.

2 Heat remaining oil and butter in a skillet. Add onion and cook for 5–7 minutes, until softened. Add garlic, cook for 1 minute. Add tomatoes, season with salt, cook for 5 minutes until tomatoes have softened.

3 Cook pasta in a large pan of boiling water, until al dente. Drain well, toss through tomato sauce. Grease a deep ovenproof dish and spread 2–3 tablespoons of the cheese mixture and half the anchovies over the bottom. Top with pasta, cover with the remaining anchovies and cheese mixture. Drizzle with olive oil, bake in the oven for 15–20 minutes, until golden.

spaghettini and scallops with breadcrumbs

ingredients

400 g (13 oz) dried spaghettini
12 fresh scallops with their corals
½ cup (125 ml, 4 fl oz) extra virgin olive oil
50 g (2 oz) fresh breadcrumbs
4 tablespoons chopped flat-leaf parsley
2 cloves garlic, minced
1 teaspoon dried chilli peppers, crushed
½ cup (125 ml, 4 fl oz) dry white wine
serves 4

1 Cook spaghettini in a large pan of boiling water, until al dente. Drain well and set aside.

2 Detach corals from scallops and set aside. Slice scallops into 3 or 4 pieces. Heat 2 tablespoons of oil in a skillet, add breadcrumbs and fry,
stirring, until golden. Remove from pan and set aside.

3 Heat remaining oil in the pan, add 2 tablespoons of parsley, the garlic and chilli. Cook for 2 minutes.

4 Add scallops and cook for 30 seconds, until starting to turn opaque. Add wine and the reserved corals, cook for a further 30 seconds, add spaghettini and cook for 1 minute, tossing to heat through. Sprinkle with breadcrumbs and remaining parsley.

preparation time
10 minutes

cooking time
15 minutes

**nutritional value
per serve**
fat: 13.7 g
carbohydrate: 35 g
protein: 8.5 g

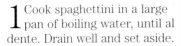

tagliatelle with tomato and mussels

ingredients

400 g (13 oz) dried tagliatelle
225 g (7½ oz) cooked shelled mussels
2 tablespoons chopped fresh basil
extra basil, for garnish

sauce

750 g (1 lb 8 oz) plum tomatoes
1 tablespoon olive oil
1 onion, finely chopped
2 cloves garlic, minced
2 stalks celery, finely chopped
1 red bell pepper, chopped
125 g (4 oz) button mushrooms,
  finely chopped
4 sun-dried tomatoes, finely chopped
½ cup (125 ml, 4 fl oz) red wine
2 tablespoons tomato puree
black pepper

serves 4

preparation time
30 minutes

cooking time
1 hour 15 minutes

**nutritional value
per serve**
fat: 1.7 g
carbohydrate: 17 g
protein: 5.6 g

1 To make sauce, cover plum tomatoes with boiling water and leave for 30 seconds. Drain, peel, seed and chop.

2 Heat oil in a pan. Add onion, garlic, celery, red bell pepper and mushrooms. Cook for 5 minutes until softened, stirring occasionally. Add chopped tomatoes, sun-dried tomatoes, red wine, tomato puree and black pepper. Bring to the boil, cover, reduce heat and simmer for 20 minutes or until vegetables are tender, stirring occasionally.

3 Cook the tagliatelle in boiling water, until al dente. Add mussels to tomato sauce, increase heat and cook, uncovered, for 5 minutes, stirring occasionally. Drain pasta, add to sauce with basil, toss well. Garnish with basil leaves and serve.

spaghetti with tuna

ingredients

3 tablespoons extra virgin olive oil
1 onion, chopped
2 cloves garlic, minced
6 anchovy fillets, drained
400 g (13 oz) can chopped tomatoes
185 g (6 oz) can tuna chunks in olive oil,
    drained and flaked
black pepper
400 g (13 oz) dried spaghetti
3 tablespoons chopped flat-leaf parsley
serves 4

i

preparation time
15 minutes

cooking time
40 minutes

**nutritional value
per serve**
fat: 7.5 g
carbohydrate: 25 g
protein: 9.1 g

1 Heat oil in a large skillet, gently cook onion for 5–7 minutes, until softened. Add garlic and anchovies, cook for 2 minutes until anchovies have broken down.

2 Increase heat, stir in tomatoes and simmer, uncovered, for 5 minutes. Add tuna and pepper. Mix well, reduce heat and simmer for 20–25 minutes, until sauce has thickened.

3 Cook the pasta in a large pan of boiling water, until al dente. Drain well. Transfer to a serving bowl, spoon over the sauce and toss well. Garnish with parsley.

linguine with shrimps and scallops

ingredients

400 g (13 oz) linguine
1 kg (2 lb) tomatoes
olive oil, for drizzling
salt and pepper
90 ml (3 fl oz) olive oil
220 g (7½ oz) scallops
220 g (7½ oz) large green shrimps,
    peeled
150 g (5 oz) squid,
    cut into rings
220 g (7½ oz) firm white fish fillet,
    cut into cubes
3 garlic cloves, minced
2 brown onions, chopped
1 tablespoon tomato paste, optional
⅓ cup (90 ml, 3 fl oz) water
2 tablespoons chopped fresh parsley
parmesan, grated
serves 4

1 Preheat oven to 180°C (350°F, gas mark 4).

2 Cook linguine in a large pan of boiling water, until al dente. Drain, set aside and keep warm. Cut the tomatoes in half and place on a baking tray. Drizzle with olive oil, sprinkle with salt and pepper, and roast in oven for 40–45 minutes.

3 Place in a food processor and process until just combined.

4 Heat oil in a large pan, sauté onion and garlic until lightly coloured. Add fish, tossing gently for 1–2 minutes. Add squid, cook 1 minute, add

scallops and shrimps, cook a further minute. Add tomato mixture, tomato paste and water and simmer for 5–10 minutes, making sure not to overcook seafood. Season with salt and pepper, stir through parsley. Serve with linguine and garnish with parmesan.

i

preparation time
15 minutes

cooking time
55 minutes

nutritional value per serve
fat: 3.8 g
carbohydrate: 12 g
protein: 7.9 g

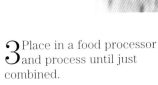

spinach, fish and ricotta cannelloni

ingredients

500 g (1 lb) cod or haddock fillet
250 g (8 oz) dried spinach lasagne
salt and black pepper
3 tablespoons butter
1 small onion, chopped
3 tablespoons all purpose flour
2 cups (500 ml, 16 fl oz) milk
1 tablespoon finely chopped fresh chives
juice of ¹/₂ lemon
30g (1 oz) frozen spinach, defrosted
250 g (8 oz) ricotta cheese
1 teaspoon chopped fresh parsley
1 teaspoon chopped fresh basil
425 g (14 oz) can chopped tomatoes
2 tablespoons fresh white breadcrumbs
2 tablespoons grated cheddar
serves 4

1 Preheat oven to 180°C (350°F, gas mark 4). Place fish in a large saucepan, cover with cold water and simmer for 10 minutes until cooked through. Flake, discarding skin and bones, and set aside. Cook lasagne for 2 minutes in boiling water. Drain, rinse and pat dry with paper towels.

preparation time
20 minutes

cooking time
30 minutes

**nutritional value
per serve**
fat: 5.4 g
carbohydrate: 5 g
protein: 7.8 g

2 Heat 1 tablespoon of butter in a pan. Gently cook onion for 2–3 minutes, until golden. Add flour and cook, stirring, for 1 minute. Remove from heat and slowly stir in milk. Return to heat, bring to the boil, stirring until thickened. Add chives, lemon juice and salt and pepper.

3 Heat remaining butter in a large pan, add fish, ricotta and herbs. Mix to combine. Squeeze any moisture from spinach and fold into fish mixture. Combine to heat through. Spoon a little mixture onto each lasagne sheet and roll into tubes. Pour tomatoes into a 10-inch square ovenproof dish. Place tubes on top, pour over white sauce and sprinkle with breadcrumbs and cheddar. Cook in the oven for 30–35 minutes, until golden.

baked rigatoni with smoked salmon

ingredients

400 g (13 oz) dried rigatoni (pasta tubes)
salt
150 g (5 oz) gruyère, grated
150 g (5 oz) cheddar, grated
2 tablespoons chopped fresh dill
200 ml (7 fl oz) crème fraîche
½ teaspoon cayenne pepper
2 tablespoons butter
250 g (8 oz) smoked salmon, cut into strips
serves 4

i

preparation time
15 minutes

cooking time
30 minutes

nutritional value
per serve
fat: 16.3 g
carbohydrate: 24 g
protein: 14.2 g

1 Preheat oven to 200°C (400°F, gas mark 6). Cook pasta in boiling water, until al dente. Drain, return to pan. Set aside 1 tablespoon each of the gruyère, cheddar and dill. Combine rest with the pasta, crème fraîche and cayenne.

2 Grease an 8 x 6 inch ovenproof dish with half the butter, spoon in half the pasta. Lay salmon strips on top and cover with remaining pasta. Sprinkle with reserved gruyère, cheddar and dill, then dot with the remaining butter. Cover with foil, bake for 15 minutes. Remove foil and bake for a further 5 minutes or until the top is bubbling and golden.

lobster lemon and dill sauce

ingredients

500 g (1 lb) spaghetti
4 green lobster tails
90 g (3 oz) butter
1 clove garlic, minced
1/2 cup (125 ml, 4 fl oz) sherry
2 tablespoons chopped fresh dill
155 ml (5 fl oz) fish stock
350 ml (11 1/2 fl oz) light cream
1 tablespoon tomato paste
salt to taste
freshly ground black pepper
juice of 1/2 lemon
extra fresh dill, chopped
serves 4

1 Cook spaghetti in a large pan of boiling water, until al dente. Drain, set aside and keep warm.

2 Remove lobster meat from shell and cut into medallions.

3 Melt butter in a skillet and sauté garlic for 1 minute. Add lobster and sauté for 1–2 minutes. Remove from pan, set aside and keep warm.

4 Add sherry and dill to skillet. Cook until liquid is reduced by half. Add fish stock, again reducing by half. Reduce heat, add cream, tomato paste, salt and pepper and simmer for 4–5 minutes.

5 Return lobster meat and juices to pan, add lemon juice and combine to heat through. Serve on spaghetti, garnish with extra dill.

preparation time
15 minutes

cooking time
20 minutes

nutritional value per serve
fat: 15.2 g
carbohydrate: 23 g
protein: 8.3 g

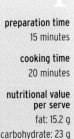

poultry

soup with mixed pastas

ingredients

1 litre (1²/₃ pints) chicken stock
1 cup (250 ml, 8 fl oz) water
3 bay leaves
1 large onion, chopped
1 large carrot, chopped
4 cloves garlic, minced
1 teaspoon olive oil
250 g (8 oz) chicken breast fillets,
    coarsely chopped
4 x 125 g (4 oz) each of pasta of choice
    (macaroni, spaghetti, shells,
    alfabetini etc)
4-6 fresh sage leaves

serves 4-6

i

preparation time
20 minutes

cooking time
25 minutes

**nutritional value
per serve**
fat: 1.3 g
carbohydrate: 16 g
protein: 5.8 g

1 In a large pan bring chicken stock and water to the boil. Add bay leaves, onion, carrot and garlic. Reduce heat and simmer, uncovered, for 10 minutes.

2 In a large skillet heat oil over medium-high heat. Add chicken and cook for 3 minutes until golden. Add cooked chicken, pastas and sage to soup mix. Simmer, uncovered, for 8–10 minutes until pasta is al dente. Discard bay leaves.

chicken minestrone

ingredients
olive oil spray
1 onion, finely chopped
1 clove garlic, minced
1 stalk celery, chopped
1 carrot, diced
425 g (14 oz) can tomatoes
1 litre (1 3/4 pints) water
freshly ground black pepper
1 teaspoon dried oregano
1 teaspoon mixed spice
2 tablespoons chopped parsley
90 g (3 oz) macaroni
1/4 cabbage, shredded
150 g (5 oz) frozen baby peas
200 g (7 oz) chicken breast fillet, sliced
serves 4-6

1 Spray base of large pan with olive oil. Add onion and garlic, cook stirring over medium heat until softened. Add celery and carrot, and cook for a further 1 minute.

2 Add tomatoes, water, pepper, oregano, spice and parsley. Bring to the boil, add macaroni, and stir until soup returns to the boil. Reduce heat and simmer for 15 minutes.

3 Stir in cabbage, peas and chicken. Simmer for a further 15–20 minutes or until chicken is tender. Serve with crusty bread.

preparation time
20 minutes

cooking time
40 minutes

nutritional value per serve
fat: 0.9 g
carbohydrate: 4 g
protein: 2.8 g

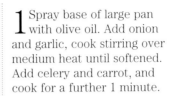

italian chicken pasta toss

ingredients

185 g (6 oz) dried pasta ribbons
2 tomatoes, seeded and chopped
1 small onion, chopped
1 small zucchini, sliced
1 small red bell pepper,
  cut into strips
250 g (8 oz) chicken breast fillets,
  cut into strips
90 g (3 oz) frozen peas
1 teaspoon salt
1 teaspoon dried italian seasoning
1 tablespoon grated parmesan

serves 4-6

i

preparation time
20 minutes

cooking time
25 minutes

nutritional value
per serve
fat: 1.7 g
carbohydrate: 12 g
protein: 7.7 g

1 Cook pasta in a large pan of boiling water, until al dente. Drain and set aside.

2 Heat oil in a large skillet, add garlic and chicken. Stir-fry on a medium heat for 5 minutes. Add onion, zucchini, bell pepper, peas and seasoning, and stir-fry a further 2 minutes. Add tomatoes, stirring for 1–2 minutes to heat through. Remove from heat, add pasta, tossing to combine. Sprinkle with parmesan.

chicken and mushroom linguine

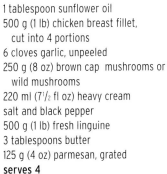

ingredients

1 tablespoon sunflower oil
500 g (1 lb) chicken breast fillet,
  cut into 4 portions
6 cloves garlic, unpeeled
250 g (8 oz) brown cap mushrooms or
  wild mushrooms
220 ml (7$\frac{1}{2}$ fl oz) heavy cream
salt and black pepper
500 g (1 lb) fresh linguine
3 tablespoons butter
125 g (4 oz) parmesan, grated
serves 4

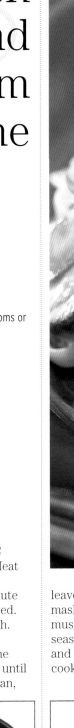

1 Preheat oven to 200°C (400°F, gas mark 6). Heat oil in a large skillet, add chicken and fry for 1 minute on each side, until browned. Place in an ovenproof dish.

2 Add garlic cloves to the pan, fry for 3 minutes until softened. Remove from pan, leave to cool slightly, peel, mash and add to chicken with mushrooms, cream and seasoning. Cover dish with foil and bake for 20 minutes until cooked.

3 Cook pasta in a large pan of boiling water, until al dente. Drain, return to the pan, toss with butter and parmesan. Serve linguine topped with chicken and mushroom mixture.

oriental chicken pasta salad

ingredients

400 g (13 oz) dried spaghetti or linguine
125 g (4 oz) baby corn
250 g (8 oz) cooked chicken, chopped
1 small cucumber, thinly sliced
1 small red or green bell pepper,
  cut into strips
1 carrot, thinly sliced
2 green onions, thinly sliced
$1/3$ cup (90 ml, 3 fl oz) tarragon vinegar
  or rice vinegar
3 tablespoons olive oil
3 tablespoons soy sauce
1 teaspoon sesame oil
$1/2$ teaspoon sugar
$1/2$ teaspoon dry mustard
dash tabasco
cilantro to garnish

serves 4-6

preparation time
25 minutes

cooking time
20 minutes

nutritional value per serve
fat: 6.8 g
carbohydrate: 25 g
protein: 9.9 g

1 Cook pasta in a large pan of boiling water, until al dente. Drain well and set aside.

2 In a large bowl combine cooked pasta, corn, chicken, cucumber, bell pepper, carrot and green onions. Toss gently to combine.

3 Combine vinegar, olive oil, soy sauce, sesame oil, sugar, mustard and tabasco in a large jar. Pour dressing over pasta mixture. Toss to coat. Serve garnished with cilantro.

rigatoni with turkey and sage ragoût

ingredients

2 tablespoons olive oil
1 onion, finely chopped
1 small red chilli pepper, seeded and
    finely chopped
1 green bell pepper, chopped
500 g (1 lb) ground turkey
220 g (7 oz) can chopped tomatoes
1 tablespoon tomato puree
salt and black pepper
50 g (2 oz) pitted black olives, sliced
2 tablespoons chopped fresh sage
500 g (1 lb) fresh rigatoni
serves 4

1 Heat oil in a large pan. Gently cook onion, chilli pepper and bell pepper, stirring, for 5 minutes until softened.

2 Add turkey, stirring to separate, cook over medium-high heat for 5 minutes, until browned. Add tomatoes, tomato puree and seasoning. Cover, reduce heat and simmer for 20 minutes. Stir in olives and half of the sage. Simmer for 2–3 minutes.

3 Cook the pasta in a large pan of boiling water, until al dente. Drain well, add to sauce and toss gently. Serve sprinkled with remaining sage.

preparation time
15 minutes

cooking time
35 minutes

**nutritional value
per serve**
fat: 4.1 g
carbohydrate: 25.5 g
protein: 13.2 g

penne with chicken sauce

ingredients

2 teaspoons ground cumin
1 teaspoon olive oil
250 g (8 oz) mushrooms, sliced
470 ml (15 fl oz) jar pasta sauce
470 ml (15 fl oz) chicken stock
15 pitted black olives, finely chopped
400 g (13 oz) precooked chicken breast,
  cut into strips
250 g (8 oz) stir-fry vegetables
  (frozen or fresh)
400 g (13 oz) dried penne

serves 4–6

1 In a large skillet heat oil, sauté cumin on a medium heat for 1 minute.

2 Add mushrooms, pasta sauce, chicken stock, olives, cooked chicken and vegetables. Cook for 5–6 minutes until vegetables are tender but crisp.

3 Cook pasta in a large pan of boiling water, until al dente. Drain well and set aside.

4 Serve pasta topped with chicken sauce.

i

preparation time
25 minutes

cooking time
20 minutes

nutritional value per serve
fat: 4.1 g
carbohydrate: 25 g
protein: 13.2 g

chicken and broccoli lasagne

ingredients

900 ml (1½ pints) milk
2 shallots, sliced
2 stalks celery, sliced
2 bay leaves
250 g (8 oz) broccoli, cut into small florets
2 tablespoons sunflower oil
1 onion, chopped
1 clove garlic, minced
250 g (8 oz) mushrooms, sliced
2 small zucchini, sliced
3 tablespoons butter
45 g (1½ oz) all purpose flour
125 g (4 oz) mature cheddar, grated
320 g (11 oz) boneless chicken breasts,
   cooked and chopped
black pepper
180 g (6 oz) egg lasagne verdi sheets
serves 4-6

1 Place milk, shallots, celery and bay leaves in a pan, bring to the boil, remove from heat, stand for 20 minutes. Strain, discard shallots, etc. and reserve infused milk.

2 Cook broccoli in boiling water for 2 minutes. Drain and set aside.

preparation time
20 minutes

cooking time
45-55 minutes

**nutritional value
per serve**
fat: 7.3 g
carbohydrate: 8.7 g
protein: 6.7 g

3 Heat oil in a large skillet, sauté onion and garlic for 2–3 minutes until softened. Add mushrooms and zucchini, cook further 4–5 minutes. Set aside.

4 Preheat oven to 180°C (350°F, gas mark 4). Melt butter in a large pan, stir in flour to make a paste, add strained milk, bring to the boil, whisking. Reduce heat, simmer for 1–2 minutes until thickened. Set aside about a third of sauce. To the remaining sauce add half of the cheese, the broccoli and mushroom mixture, chopped chicken and black pepper.

5 Spoon half of the mixture into a shallow ovenproof dish. Top with half the lasagne sheets. Repeat and pour over reserved sauce, sprinkle with remaining cheese. Bake for 40–45 minutes, until golden and bubbling.

quick chicken lasagne

ingredients

500 g (1 lb) chicken thigh fillets
salt and pepper
375 g (12¹/₂ oz) jar tomato pasta sauce
250 g (8 oz) instant lasagne sheets
100 g (3¹/₂ oz) mushrooms, sliced
topping
250 g (8 oz) ricotta
210 g (7 oz) plain yogurt
2 tablespoons romano or parmesan,
  grated
pinch nutmeg
2 eggs, lightly beaten
extra parmesan, to serve
serves 6

1 Preheat oven to 180°C (350°F, gas mark 4). Place thigh fillets between 2 pieces of plastic wrap and pound out with a meat mallet until thin. Season with salt and pepper.

2 Grease a large baking dish with oil. Spread a thin layer of tomato sauce over the bottom. Wet 4 lasagne sheets

and place on top of sauce. Spread with tomato sauce. Place thigh fillets over the tomato sauce in a single layer and cover with sliced mushrooms. Wet another 4 lasagne sheets and lay over mushrooms. Spread remaining tomato sauce over lasagne sheets.

3 Combine topping ingredients in a large bowl, mix well. Spread over the lasagne. Sprinkle with extra parmesan, bake for 35–40 minutes, until golden and bubbling.

4 Stand for 10 minutes before serving.

i

preparation time
20 minutes

cooking time
45-50 minutes

nutritional value per serve
fat: 5.2 g
carbohydrate: 11.6 g
protein: 10.7 g

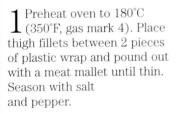

fruited chicken pasta salad

ingredients

250 g (8 oz) dried macaroni
250 g (8 oz) cooked chicken or turkey,
    chopped
320 g (11 oz) can tangerine or
    mandarin orange pieces
180 g (6 oz) seedless grapes, halved
1 stalk celery, sliced
$\frac{1}{2}$ cup (125 ml, 4 fl oz) ranch-style salad
    dressing
pinch of pepper
1-2 tablespoons milk
4-5 iceberg lettuce leaves
250 g (8 oz) can water chestnuts, sliced

serves 4-6

preparation time
15 minutes

cooking time
20 minutes

**nutritional value
per serve**
fat: 3.8 g
carbohydrate: 18 g
protein: 6.8 g

1 Cook pasta in a large pan of boiling water, until al dente. Drain well and set aside.

2 In a large bowl combine cooked pasta, chicken or turkey, tangerines, grapes, water chestnuts and celery. Set aside.

3 In a small bowl combine ranch dressing and pepper. Pour over chicken mixture and toss lightly to coat.

4 Before serving, if necessary, stir in a little milk to moisten. Serve with lettuce cups.

glossary

al dente: Italian term to describe pasta and rice that are cooked until tender but still firm to the bite.

bake blind: to bake pastry cases without their fillings. Line the raw pastry case with wax paper and fill with raw rice or dried beans to prevent collapsed sides and puffed base. Remove paper and fill 5 minutes before completion of cooking time.

baste: to spoon hot cooking liquid over food at intervals during cooking to moisten and flavor it.

beat: to make a mixture smooth with rapid and regular motions using a spatula, wire whisk or electric mixer; to make a mixture light and smooth by enclosing air.

beurre manié: equal quantities of butter and flour mixed together to a smooth paste and stirred little by little into a soup, stew or sauce while on the heat to thicken. Stop adding when desired thickness results.

bind: to add egg or a thick sauce to hold ingredients together when cooked.

blanch: to plunge some foods into boiling water for less than a minute and immediately plunge into iced water. This is to brighten the color of some vegetables; to remove skin from tomatoes and nuts.

blend: to mix 2 or more ingredients thoroughly together; do not confuse with blending in an electric blender.

boil: to cook in a liquid brought to boiling point and kept there.

boiling point: when bubbles rise continually and break over the entire surface of the liquid, reaching a temperature of 100°C (212°F). In some cases food is held at this high temperature for a few seconds then heat is turned to low for slower cooking. See simmer.

bouquet garni: a bundle of several herbs tied together with string for easy removal, placed into pots of stock, soups and stews for flavor. A few sprigs of fresh thyme, parsley and bay leaf are used. Can be purchased in sachet form for convenience.

caramelize: to heat sugar in a heavy pan until it liquefies and develops a caramel color. Vegetables such as blanched carrots and sautéed onions may be sprinkled with sugar and caramelized.

chill: to place in the refrigerator or stir over ice until cold.

clarify: to make a liquid clear by removing sediments and impurities. To melt fat and remove any sediment.

coat: to dust or roll food items in flour to cover the surface before the food is cooked. Also, to coat in flour, egg and breadcrumbs.

cool: to stand at room temperature until some or all heat is removed, e.g., cool a little, cool completely.

cream: to make creamy and fluffy by working the mixture with the back of a wooden spoon, usually refers to creaming butter and sugar or margarine. May also be creamed with an electric mixer.

croutons: small cubes of bread, toasted or fried, used as an addition to salads or as a garnish to soups and stews.

crudite: raw vegetable sticks served with a dipping sauce.

crumb: to coat foods in flour, egg and breadcrumbs to form a protective coating for foods that are fried. Also adds flavor, texture and enhances appearance.

cube: to cut into small pieces with six even sides, e.g., cubes of meat.

cut in: to combine fat and flour using 2 knives scissor fashion or with a pastry blender, to make pastry.

deglaze: to dissolve dried out cooking juices left on the bottom and sides of a roasting dish or skillet. Add a little water, wine or stock, scrape and stir over heat until dissolved. Resulting liquid is used to make a flavorsome gravy or added to a sauce or casserole.

degrease: to skim fat from the surface of cooking liquids, e.g., stocks, soups, casseroles.

dice: to cut into small cubes.

dredge: to heavily coat with powdered sugar, sugar, flour or cornstarch.

dressing: a mixture added to completed dishes to add moisture and flavor, e.g., salads, cooked vegetables.

drizzle: to pour in a fine thread-like stream moving over a surface.

egg wash: beaten egg with milk or water used to brush over pastry, bread dough or cookies to give a sheen and golden brown color.

essence: a strong flavoring liquid, usually made by distillation. Only a few drops are needed to flavor.

fillet: a piece of prime meat, fish or poultry that is boneless or has all bones removed.

flake: to separate cooked fish into flakes, removing any bones and skin, using 2 forks.

flame: to ignite warmed alcohol over food or to pour into a pan with food, ignite then serve.

flute: to make decorative indentations around the pastry edge before baking.

fold in: combining of a light, whipped or creamed mixture with other ingredients. Add a portion of the other ingredients at a time and mix using a gentle circular motion, over and under the mixture so that air will not be lost. Use a silver spoon or spatula.

glaze: to brush or coat food with a liquid that will give the finished product a glossy appearance, and on baked products, a golden brown color.

grease: to rub the surface of a metal or heatproof dish with oil or fat, to prevent the food from sticking.

herbed butter: softened butter mixed with finely chopped fresh herbs and re-chilled. Used to serve on grilled meats and fish.

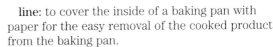

hors d'ouvre: small savory foods served as an appetizer, popularly known today as "finger food".

infuse: to steep foods in a liquid until the liquid absorbs their flavor.

joint: to cut poultry and game into serving pieces by dividing at the joint.

julienne: to cut some food, e.g., vegetables and processed meats into fine strips the length of matchsticks. Used for inclusion in salads or as a garnish to cooked dishes.

knead: to work a yeast dough in a pressing, stretching and folding motion with the heel of the hand until smooth and elastic to develop the gluten strands. Non-yeast doughs should be lightly and quickly handled as gluten development is not desired.

line: to cover the inside of a baking pan with paper for the easy removal of the cooked product from the baking pan.

macerate: to stand fruit in a syrup, liqueur or spirit to give added flavor.

marinade: a flavored liquid, into which food is placed for some time to give it flavor and to tenderize. Marinades include an acid ingredient such as vinegar or wine, oil and seasonings.

mask: to evenly cover cooked food portions with a sauce, mayonnaise or savory jelly.

pan-fry: to fry foods in a small amount of fat or oil, sufficient to coat the bottom of the pan.

parboil: to boil until partially cooked. The food is then finished by some other method.

pare: to peel the skin from vegetables and fruit. Peel is the popular term but pare is the name given to the knife used; paring knife.

pith: the white lining between the rind and flesh of oranges, grapefruit and lemons.

pit: to remove stones or seeds from olives, cherries, dates.

pitted: the olives, cherries, dates, etc., with the stone removed, e.g., purchase pitted dates.

poach: to simmer gently in enough hot liquid to almost cover the food so shape will be retained.

pound: to flatten meats with a meat mallet; to reduce to a paste or small particles with a mortar and pestle.

simmer: to cook in liquid just below boiling point at about 96°C (205°F) with small bubbles rising gently to the surface.

skim: to remove fat or froth from the surface of simmering food.

stock: the liquid produced when meat, poultry, fish or vegetables have been simmered in water to extract the flavor. Used as a base for soups, sauces, casseroles, etc. Convenience stock products are available.

sweat: to cook sliced onions or vegetables, in a small amount of butter in a covered pan over low heat, to soften them and release flavor without coloring.

conversions

measurements differ from country to country, so it's important to understand what the differences are. This Measurements Guide gives you simple "at-a-glance" information for using the recipes in this book, wherever you may be.

Cooking is not an exact science – minor variations in measurements won't make a difference to your cooking.

equipment

There is a difference in the size of measuring cups used internationally, but the difference is minimal (only 2–3 teaspoons). We use the Australian standard metric measurements in our recipes:

1 teaspoon ....5 ml   1 tablespoon....20 ml
½ cup......125 ml   1 cup.....250 ml
4 cups...1 liter

Measuring cups come in sets of one cup (250 ml), ½ cup (125 ml), ⅓ cup (80 ml) and ¼ cup (60 ml). Use these for measuring liquids and certain dry ingredients.

Measuring spoons come in a set of four and should be used for measuring dry and liquid ingredients.

When using cup or spoon measures always make them level (unless the recipe indicates otherwise).

dry versus wet ingredients

While this system of measures is consistent for liquids, it's more difficult to quantify dry ingredients. For instance, one level cup equals: 200 g of brown sugar; 210 g of superfine sugar; and 110 g of powdered sugar.

When measuring dry ingredients such as flour, don't push the flour down or shake it into the cup. It is best just to spoon the flour in until it reaches the desired amount. When measuring liquids use a clear vessel indicating metric levels.

Always use medium eggs (1.5-2.5 oz) when eggs are required in a recipe.

dry

metric (grams)	imperial (ounces)
30 g	1 oz
60 g	2 oz
90 g	3 oz
100 g	3½ oz
125 g	4 oz
150 g	5 oz
185 g	6 oz
200 g	7 oz
250 g	8 oz
280 g	9 oz
315 g	10 oz
330 g	11 oz
370 g	12 oz
400 g	13 oz
440 g	14 oz
470 g	15 oz
500 g	16 oz (1 lb)
750 g	24 oz (1½ lb)
1000 g (1 kg)	32 oz (2 lb)

liquids

metric (milliliters)	imperial (fluid ounces)
30 ml	1 fl oz
60 ml	2 fl oz
90 ml	3 fl oz
100 ml	3½ fl oz
125 ml	4 fl oz
150 ml	5 fl oz
190 ml	6 fl oz
250 ml	8 fl oz
300 ml	10 fl oz
500 ml	16 fl oz
600 ml	20 fl oz (1 pint)*
1000 ml (1 liter)	32 fl oz

*Note: an American pint is 16 fl oz.

oven

Your oven should always be at the right temperature before placing the food in it to be cooked. Note that if your oven doesn't have a fan you may need to cook food for a little longer.

microwave

It is difficult to give an exact cooking time for microwave cooking. It is best to watch what you are cooking closely to monitor its progress.

standing time

Many foods continue to cook when you take them out of the oven or microwave. If a recipe states that the food needs to "stand" after cooking, be sure not to overcook the dish.

can sizes

The can sizes available in your supermarket or grocery store may not be the same as specified in the recipe. Don't worry if there is a small variation in size—it's unlikely to make a difference to the end result.

cooking temperatures	°C (celsius)	°F (fahrenheit)	gas mark
very slow	120	250	1/2
slow	150	300	2
moderately slow	160	315	2-3
moderate	180	350	4
moderate hot	190	375	5
	200	400	6
hot	220	425	7
very hot	230	450	8
	240	475	9
	250	500	10

index